LeGon Suits Up!

Fulton Books
Meadville, PA

Published by Fulton Books 2023

ISBN 979-8-88982-064-2 (paperback)
ISBN 979-8-88982-066-6 (hardcover)
ISBN 979-8-88982-065-9 (digital)

Printed in the United States of America

LeGon Suits Up!

Dr. Karen Campbell Kuebler

Chicago, Illinois, 1916
Here comes Jeni LeGon
on the scene.

She loved to perform for children in town.
The stoop was for the audience,
and Jeni danced around.

At fifteen, Jeni danced in the Whitman Sisters' show.

Jeni did the snakehips dance with Alice and Catherine in a row.

In 1935, Jeni and
Bojangles danced away.
Over one thousand dollars
per week was her pay.

New York's Harlem
was Jeni's favorite space.
She rode her bicycle
from place to place.

As the first black woman
to dance on screen,

Jeni's Charleston, Truckin', and Rumba were the best anyone had ever seen.

12

Fats Waller played the
piano while Jeni rolled
her eyes and tapped.

14

By 1938, Ms. LeGon performed
in London in a white
tuxedo and top hat.
No one ever saw a woman
dress and dance like that.

Off to Vancouver, Canada
for 20 years to teach dance.
Ms. LeGon loved giving students a chance.

**Jeni LeGon's
dancing spirit
lives in you!**

Wear pants and dance
your whole life through.

References

Frank, R. 1994. *Tap! The Greatest Tap Dance Stars and Their Stories: 1900-1955.* New York, NY: De Capo Press Inc.

George-Graves, N. (2018). Identity Politics and Political Will: Jeni Legon Living in a Great Big Way. In J. R. Giersdorf & Y. Wong (Eds.), The Routledge Dance Studies Reader (pp. 297–314). Routledge.

Jackson, F. "LeGon Dances a Sensation in New Cantor Film." 1937. *The California Eagle.* August 22, 1937.

Malone, J. 1996. *Steppin' on the blues: The Visible Rhythms of African American Dance.* Chicago, IL: University of Illinois Press.

Mann, M. "Going Hollywood." 1935. *The Leader.* August 8, 1935.

Morris, E. "Maxine 'Wows' 'Em on L.A.'s Central Avenue." *The Pittsburgh Courier.* August 13, 1938.

Perron, W. (2022, January 22). *Jeni Legon (1916–2012).* WENDY PERRON. Retrieved April 2, 2023, from https://wendyperron.com/jeni-legon-1916-2012/

Seibert, B. 2015. *What the Eye Hears: A History of Tap Dancing.* New York, NY: Farrar, Straus, and Giroux.

About the Author

Karen started dancing at the age of three and never stops moving. She has always loved reading biographies and dancing stories. A passion for dance history developed in college and continues to inspire her research. As a mom and teacher, Karen enjoys creating customized songs and dances for everything you can imagine. She also loves exploring nature (especially making snow angels), traveling (especially to francophone countries), and laughing with friends. Karen lives in Baltimore, Maryland, with her husband, Brian, lots of books, and lots of props for story dances.